She reads WORD

How TO:

Over the next month, take each day to read a scripture passage, whether one verse or a chapter. I would advise you not to review too much at once to have time to take in all the scripture has to offer. This will allow you time to get an understanding and for God to release wisdom to you from what you've read in relation to His nature and your personal faith.

To enrich your Bible study experience, try referencing three different versions of the Bible and note the date. This can include the entire passage or simply the name of the book and its corresponding verses. Additionally, research the **author** of the book, the date **when** it was written, and its intended **audience**.

In the **Thought Box,** jot down quick notes that come to mind during your reading. This could involve past experiences, personal connections, or even drawing images if words fail to express the emotion.

Definition/ REFLECTION & REVELATION

Scripture contains many words that extend beyond our common knowledge. Take the time to note any words that you don't fully grasp or want to learn more about their ***definition***. Understanding the contextual definition as per scripture can provide a deeper level of clarity and revelation.

After completing your research and compiling notes, it's important to ***reflect*** on your work. Take a moment to allow the word of God to examine you and note your ***personal reflections***. Take a deep breath and invite the Holy Spirit to speak to you. Everyone experiences communication from God differently - some may hear Him audibly, while others may have an inner knowing or thoughts that seem like their own. Some may even have visions or dreams that help them understand what they've read.

Be patient in this process of learning how you hear from God. It may take a few days but continue to ***reflect*** on what you've read. The more you practice these study strategies the easier it will be to identify how you hear from God.

Take time to write detailed notes of your ***thoughts***, ***feelings***, and ***emotions*** in relation to your study passage. All of this is relevant to growing in your faith and relationship with God. Maturing in your study will help you identify why you felt some kind of way while reading. You may even be able to understand these aspects of yourself sooner rather than later.

Studying the Bible is a multifaceted experience. Enjoy every twist and turn. May the peace of God be with you and may the eyes of your understanding be enlightened.

Happy STUDIES

Jessica McNeil

Prayer

God thank you the person holding this book. I ask that you create in them a clean heart and renew your right spirit in them. Remove scales from their eyes and unstop their ears from any blockages that will hinder them from hearing from you with clarity. Release keen sight and hearing by your spirit. Enlighten the eyes of their understanding that complex things will be made plain to them. Help them to hear your voice and receive wisdom, knowledge, and understanding. God make yourself known to them and help them to encounter in a new way.

Father release your nature and character through your word. Lord fill the space where they study with an atmosphere conducive to your presence. In that place, God have your way in them. Release fresh revelation with each moment in your presence. They will be one that will rightly divide your word of truth.

Bless each woman as *She* reads **WORD!** In your name Jesus, amen.

Today's verse

DATE ____________

SCRIPTURE:

WHO WROTE IT ?

WHO IS IT WRITTEN TO ?

CHOOSE 3 BIBLE VERSIONS TO REFERENCE

THOUGHT BOX

DEFINITION

Personal Reflection

Did you learn something new?

How do you relate to this?

Would you continue to read further?

What is your biggest takeaway?

Thoughts / Revelations

Thoughts / Revelations

Thoughts / Revelations

Today's verse

DATE ____________

SCRIPTURE:

WHO WROTE IT ?

WHO IS IT WRITTEN TO ?

CHOOSE 3 BIBLE VERSIONS TO REFERENCE

THOUGHT BOX

DEFINITION

Personal Reflection

Did you learn something new?

How do you relate to this?

Would you continue to read further?

What is your biggest takeaway?

Thoughts / Revelations

Thoughts / Revelations

Thoughts / Revelations

Today's verse

DATE ____________

SCRIPTURE:

WHO WROTE IT ?

WHO IS IT WRITTEN TO ?

CHOOSE 3 BIBLE VERSIONS TO REFERENCE

THOUGHT BOX

DEFINITION

Personal Reflection

Did you learn something new?

How do you relate to this?

Would you continue to read further?

What is your biggest takeaway?

Thoughts / Revelations

Thoughts / Revelations

Thoughts / Revelations

Today's verse

DATE ____________

SCRIPTURE:

WHO WROTE IT ?

WHO IS IT WRITTEN TO ?

CHOOSE 3 BIBLE VERSIONS TO REFERENCE

THOUGHT BOX

DEFINITION

Personal Reflection

Did you learn something new?

How do you relate to this?

Would you continue to read further?

What is your biggest takeaway?

Thoughts / Revelations

Thoughts / Revelations

Thoughts / Revelations

Today's verse

DATE ____________

SCRIPTURE:

WHO WROTE IT ?

WHO IS IT WRITTEN TO ?

CHOOSE 3 BIBLE VERSIONS TO REFERENCE

THOUGHT BOX

DEFINITION

Personal Reflection

Did you learn something new?

How do you relate to this?

Would you continue to read further?

What is your biggest takeaway?

Thoughts / Revelations

Thoughts / Revelations

Thoughts / Revelations

Today's verse

DATE ____________

SCRIPTURE:

WHO WROTE IT ?

WHO IS IT WRITTEN TO ?

CHOOSE 3 BIBLE VERSIONS TO REFERENCE

THOUGHT BOX

DEFINITION

30

Personal Reflection

Did you learn something new?

How do you relate to this?

Would you continue to read further?

What is your biggest takeaway?

Thoughts / Revelations

Thoughts /Revelations

Thoughts / Revelations

Today's verse

DATE ____________

SCRIPTURE:

WHO WROTE IT ?

WHO IS IT WRITTEN TO ?

CHOOSE 3 BIBLE VERSIONS TO REFERENCE

THOUGHT BOX

DEFINITION

Personal Reflection

Did you learn something new?

How do you relate to this?

Would you continue to read further?

What is your biggest takeaway?

Thoughts / Revelations

Thoughts /Revelations

Thoughts / Revelations

Today's verse

D A T E ____________

SCRIPTURE:

WHO WROTE IT ?

WHO IS IT WRITTEN TO ?

CHOOSE 3 BIBLE VERSIONS TO REFERENCE

THOUGHT BOX

DEFINITION

Personal Reflection

Did you learn something new?

How do you relate to this?

Would you continue to read further?

What is your biggest takeaway?

Thoughts / Revelations

Thoughts / Revelations

Thoughts / Revelations

Today's verse

DATE ____________

SCRIPTURE:

WHO WROTE IT ?

WHO IS IT WRITTEN TO ?

CHOOSE 3 BIBLE VERSIONS TO REFERENCE

THOUGHT BOX

DEFINITION

Personal Reflection

Did you learn something new?

How do you relate to this?

Would you continue to read further?

What is your biggest takeaway?

Thoughts / Revelations

Thoughts / Revelations

Thoughts / Revelations

Today's verse

DATE ____________

SCRIPTURE:

WHO WROTE IT ?

WHO IS IT WRITTEN TO ?

CHOOSE 3 BIBLE VERSIONS TO REFERENCE

THOUGHT BOX

DEFINITION

Personal Reflection

Did you learn something new?

How do you relate to this?

Would you continue to read further?

What is your biggest takeaway?

Thoughts / Revelations

Today's verse

DATE ____________

SCRIPTURE:

WHO WROTE IT ?

WHO IS IT WRITTEN TO ?

CHOOSE 3 BIBLE VERSIONS TO REFERENCE

THOUGHT BOX

DEFINITION

Personal Reflection

Did you learn something new?

How do you relate to this?

Would you continue to read further?

What is your biggest takeaway?

Thoughts / Revelations

Thoughts / Revelations

Thoughts / Revelations

Today's verse

DATE ____________

SCRIPTURE:

WHO WROTE IT ?

WHO IS IT WRITTEN TO ?

CHOOSE 3 BIBLE VERSIONS TO REFERENCE

THOUGHT BOX

DEFINITION

Personal Reflection

Did you learn something new?

How do you relate to this?

Would you continue to read further?

What is your biggest takeaway?

Thoughts / Revelations

Thoughts / Revelations

Thoughts / Revelations

Today's verse

DATE ____________

SCRIPTURE:

WHO WROTE IT ?

WHO IS IT WRITTEN TO ?

CHOOSE 3 BIBLE VERSIONS TO REFERENCE

THOUGHT BOX

DEFINITION

Personal Reflection

Did you learn something new?

How do you relate to this?

Would you continue to read further?

What is your biggest takeaway?

Thoughts / Revelations

Thoughts / Revelations

Thoughts/Revelations

Today's verse

DATE ____________

SCRIPTURE:

WHO WROTE IT ?

WHO IS IT WRITTEN TO ?

CHOOSE 3 BIBLE VERSIONS TO REFERENCE

THOUGHT BOX

DEFINITION

Personal Reflection

Did you learn something new?

How do you relate to this?

Would you continue to read further?

What is your biggest takeaway?

Thoughts / Revelations

Thoughts / Revelations

Thoughts / Revelations

Today's verse

DATE ____________

SCRIPTURE:

WHO WROTE IT ?

WHO IS IT WRITTEN TO ?

CHOOSE 3 BIBLE VERSIONS TO REFERENCE

THOUGHT BOX

DEFINITION

Personal Reflection

Did you learn something new?

How do you relate to this?

Would you continue to read further?

What is your biggest takeaway?

Thoughts/Revelations

Thoughts/Revelations

Thoughts/Revelations

Today's verse

DATE ____________

SCRIPTURE:

WHO WROTE IT ?

WHO IS IT WRITTEN TO ?

CHOOSE 3 BIBLE VERSIONS TO REFERENCE

THOUGHT BOX

DEFINITION

Personal Reflection

Did you learn something new?

How do you relate to this?

Would you continue to read further?

What is your biggest takeaway?

Thoughts/Revelations

Thoughts/Revelations

Thoughts/Revelations

Today's verse

DATE ____________

SCRIPTURE:

WHO WROTE IT ?

WHO IS IT WRITTEN TO ?

CHOOSE 3 BIBLE VERSIONS TO REFERENCE

THOUGHT BOX

DEFINITION

Personal Reflection

Did you learn something new?

How do you relate to this?

Would you continue to read further?

What is your biggest takeaway?

Thoughts/Revelations

Thoughts/Revelations

Thoughts/Revelations

Today's verse

DATE ____________

SCRIPTURE:

WHO WROTE IT ?

WHO IS IT WRITTEN TO ?

CHOOSE 3 BIBLE VERSIONS TO REFERENCE

THOUGHT BOX

DEFINITION

Personal Reflection

Did you learn something new?

How do you relate to this?

Would you continue to read further?

What is your biggest takeaway?

Thoughts/ Revelations

Thoughts/Revelations

Thoughts/Revelations

Today's verse

DATE ______________

SCRIPTURE:

WHO WROTE IT ?

WHO IS IT WRITTEN TO ?

CHOOSE 3 BIBLE VERSIONS TO REFERENCE

THOUGHT BOX

DEFINITION

Personal Reflection

Did you learn something new?

How do you relate to this?

Would you continue to read further?

What is your biggest takeaway?

Thoughts/Revelations

Thoughts/Revelations

Thoughts/Revelations

Today's verse

DATE ____________

SCRIPTURE:

WHO WROTE IT ?

WHO IS IT WRITTEN TO ?

CHOOSE 3 BIBLE VERSIONS TO REFERENCE

THOUGHT BOX

DEFINITION

Personal Reflection

Did you learn something new?

How do you relate to this?

Would you continue to read further?

What is your biggest takeaway?

Thoughts/Revelations

Thoughts/Revelations

Thoughts/Revelations

Today's verse

DATE ____________

SCRIPTURE:

WHO WROTE IT ?

WHO IS IT WRITTEN TO ?

CHOOSE 3 BIBLE VERSIONS TO REFERENCE

THOUGHT BOX

DEFINITION

Personal Reflection

Did you learn something new?

How do you relate to this?

Would you continue to read further?

What is your biggest takeaway?

Thoughts/Revelations

Thoughts/ Revelations

Thoughts/Revelations

Today's verse

DATE ____________

SCRIPTURE:

WHO WROTE IT ?

WHO IS IT WRITTEN TO ?

CHOOSE 3 BIBLE VERSIONS TO REFERENCE

THOUGHT BOX

DEFINITION

108

Personal Reflection

Did you learn something new?

How do you relate to this?

Would you continue to read further?

What is your biggest takeaway?

Thoughts/Revelations

Thoughts/Revelations

Thoughts/Revelations

Today's verse

DATE ____________

SCRIPTURE:

WHO WROTE IT ?

WHO IS IT WRITTEN TO ?

CHOOSE 3 BIBLE VERSIONS TO REFERENCE

THOUGHT BOX

DEFINITION

Personal Reflection

Did you learn something new?

How do you relate to this?

Would you continue to read further?

What is your biggest takeaway?

Thoughts/Revelations

Thoughts/Revelations

Thoughts/Revelations

Today's verse

DATE ____________

SCRIPTURE:

WHO WROTE IT ?

WHO IS IT WRITTEN TO ?

CHOOSE 3 BIBLE VERSIONS TO REFERENCE

THOUGHT BOX

DEFINITION

Personal Reflection

Did you learn something new?

How do you relate to this?

Would you continue to read further?

What is your biggest takeaway?

Thoughts/ Revelations

Thoughts/Revelations

Thoughts/Revelations

Today's verse

DATE ____________

SCRIPTURE:

WHO WROTE IT ?

WHO IS IT WRITTEN TO ?

CHOOSE 3 BIBLE VERSIONS TO REFERENCE

THOUGHT BOX

DEFINITION

Personal Reflection

Did you learn something new?

How do you relate to this?

Would you continue to read further?

What is your biggest takeaway?

Thoughts/Revelations

Thoughts/Revelations

Thoughts/Revelations

Today's verse

DATE ____________

SCRIPTURE:

WHO WROTE IT ?

WHO IS IT WRITTEN TO ?

CHOOSE 3 BIBLE VERSIONS TO REFERENCE

THOUGHT BOX

DEFINITION

128

Personal Reflection

Did you learn something new?

How do you relate to this?

Would you continue to read further?

What is your biggest takeaway?

Thoughts/Revelations

Thoughts/Revelations

Thoughts/Revelations

Today's verse

DATE ____________

SCRIPTURE:

WHO WROTE IT ?

WHO IS IT WRITTEN TO ?

CHOOSE 3 BIBLE VERSIONS TO REFERENCE

THOUGHT BOX

DEFINITION

Personal Reflection

Did you learn something new?

How do you relate to this?

Would you continue to read further?

What is your biggest takeaway?

Thoughts/Revelations

Thoughts/Revelations

Thoughts/Revelations

Today's verse

DATE ____________

SCRIPTURE:

WHO WROTE IT ?

WHO IS IT WRITTEN TO ?

CHOOSE 3 BIBLE VERSIONS TO REFERENCE

THOUGHT BOX

DEFINITION

Personal Reflection

Did you learn something new?

How do you relate to this?

Would you continue to read further?

What is your biggest takeaway?

Thoughts/Revelations

Thoughts/Revelations

Thoughts/Revelations

Today's verse

DATE ______

SCRIPTURE:

WHO WROTE IT ?

WHO IS IT WRITTEN TO ?

CHOOSE 3 BIBLE VERSIONS TO REFERENCE

THOUGHT BOX

DEFINITION

143

Personal Reflection

Did you learn something new?

How do you relate to this?

Would you continue to read further?

What is your biggest takeaway?

Thoughts/Revelations

Thoughts/Revelations

Thoughts/Revelations

Today's verse

DATE ____________

SCRIPTURE:

WHO WROTE IT ?

WHO IS IT WRITTEN TO ?

CHOOSE 3 BIBLE VERSIONS TO REFERENCE

THOUGHT BOX

DEFINITION

Personal Reflection

Did you learn something new?

How do you relate to this?

Would you continue to read further?

What is your biggest takeaway?

Thoughts/Revelations

Thoughts/Revelations

Thoughts/Revelations

Today's verse

DATE ______________

SCRIPTURE:

WHO WROTE IT ?

WHO IS IT WRITTEN TO ?

CHOOSE 3 BIBLE VERSIONS TO REFERENCE

THOUGHT BOX

DEFINITION

Personal Reflection

Did you learn something new?

How do you relate to this?

Would you continue to read further?

What is your biggest takeaway?

Thoughts/Revelations

Thoughts/Revelations

Thoughts/Revelations

Moving Forward

As you delve deeper into reading and understanding scripture, you will witness the Word of God expanding your knowledge of His character and nature. Your faith will strengthen, and you will recognize the power that God has vested in you to spread His truth to others.

Take what you've learned through your studies and apply it. Begin by praying and speaking the word of God, and allow His light to shine through you. As people observe your actions, it will create an opportunity for you to share the glory of God and the power of His word.

Greatness awaits!

→

Let's *connect*

JMCNEILLIGHT.COM

@ jmcneillight

@ jmcneillight

@ jmcneillight

@ JMcNeil_Light

Other Published Works

Before You Speak: Understanding the Power of Words

Graced for the Win: Tip for Marketing & Ministry

Watch Your Mouth | 10week Devotional
& Guided Journal

She reads WORD | Bible Study Journal

Jessica McNeil

Made in the USA
Columbia, SC
17 August 2023

21653914R00088